Narcissism

Abuse By Gas lighting And Narcissism Healing, Divorce, And Recovery From A Narcissist, Seek Refuge From Detrimental Emotional Connections And Borderline Personalities

(A Comprehensive, Step By Step Manual For Altering Abusive And Manipulative Conduct)

Domenic Larose

TABLE OF CONTENT

Effect On Cultural Standards.. 1

Managing Relationships With Narcissists.............. 7

Accepting Your Vulnerability....................................24

The Drug Of The Narcissist..42

Strategies For Handling A Narcissistic Parent....64

Handling A Narcissist..81

Various Narcissist Types 102

Breaking Free: Taking Back Your Identity........ 122

Effect On Cultural Standards

Examples of the effects this can have on society are shown below:

Normalization of narcissism: Narcissistic personalities that are portrayed as endearing or prosperous may unintentionally normalize narcissistic conduct in mainstream culture. People might start to identify narcissism with accomplishment and success, which could encourage more people to take on narcissistic characteristics.

Empathy erosion: The ubiquity of narcissistic characters in popular culture and real life may factor in society's loss of empathy. Empathy can harm how people relate to one another and deal with social concerns if it is not appreciated or encouraged.

Manipulative models: People may unintentionally learn manipulative techniques via the depiction of egotistical, manipulative individuals. Both in personal and professional contexts, this may have negative effects.

Gender stereotype reinforcement: Narcissistic personalities have the potential to perpetuate gender stereotypes, including the "alpha male" and "queen bee" archetypes. These misconceptions may hamper opportunities for more inclusive and fair social standards.

Effect on mental health: People may feel under pressure to live up to these inflated expectations of achievement and self-worth as a result of the glorification of narcissistic qualities.

Social division: Narcissistic individuals frequently put their interests ahead of everyone else's, which can cause strife and division in society. A selfish pursuit of self-interest at the expense of the common good can impede development.

In real life, as much as in media, narcissistic archetypal characters are common, and their recurrent characteristics can have a big impact on social norms. Even though they can provide interesting narratives, evaluating how they are portrayed critically is important, and considering how they affect our understanding of and reactions to narcissistic behavior in our personal and larger social contexts is important.

As we round off this chapter, we find ourselves at the nexus of self-discovery and societal knowledge. The stories we've unearthed have dipped us into the complex web of narcissism, revealing its various dimensions and the significant effects it has on both people and societies. We've seen the attraction and poisonous nature of narcissistic stories, and we know how they have the power to captivate, control, and eventually change the way we see the world.

However, we have also discovered hope in these chronicles: the strength of knowledge and self-awareness.

Remember that, like a prism; narcissism refracts light in various ways via the various cultures that define our world as we turn the page and begin the new chapter. We will examine the fascinating relationship between narcissism and culture, focusing on how the narcissistic forces at work are both affected and influenced by cultural norms, values, and beliefs.

Five Important Things to Remember

Myths and tales have frequently acted as windows reflecting facets of human nature throughout history. Stories about narcissistic individuals, like the Greek myth of Narcissus, have shed light on the intricacies of self-obsession. These tales serve as a reminder that narcissism is an enduring aspect of human nature rather than a creation of the contemporary era.

Examining how other cultures have construed and incorporated narcissistic characteristics into their narratives and worldviews presents a special chance to learn more. It enables us to understand how, throughout history, different communities have both praised and discouraged narcissism as a concept.

Narcissistic stereotypes, such as the gorgeous but emotionally aloof hero or the charming but self-absorbed villain, still impact culture and storytelling today. Acknowledge these archetypes in the characters you come across in films, TV series, and novels, and engage in introspection and empathy exercises.

When narcissistic traits are glamorized or normalized in books and other media, it can have an impact on social norms and values. Are there any examples that come to mind where the exaltation of narcissism has had negative outcomes? We must look for better behaviors and role models.

Narcissism is an essential first step toward self-improvement and self-discovery. Evaluate your actions and interactions with others, providing and cultivating humility, empathy, and sincere connection as countermeasures to narcissistic tendencies.

Managing Relationships With Narcissists

There are plenty of good reasons to decide to stick with a narcissistic spouse. Children, a lengthy marriage, combined investments, one or more businesses, insecurity, and a lack of post-divorce financial support are a few. For your emotional and mental health, you need to learn how to manage these relationships regardless of why you choose to stay with your spouse.

Your happiness, calm, and vitality are all sapped when you're with a narcissistic spouse. It is tiresome to keep trying in vain to win this individual over, with little to no progress and few improvements. When you think you've come a long way, you've only gone ten steps back to where you were ten years ago. So, if you decide to remain with your narcissistic partner, how can you maintain your sanity?

Modify Your Expectations

You need to start by lowering your expectations. You must keep it light since you already know they can't be intimate emotionally. Limit your conversation to banal subjects like the weather, your aspirations as a couple, and your weekend or date night plans. Recognize that they cannot satisfy your emotional requirements for empathy, understanding, or compassion. They would not know where to start since they cannot navigate their emotional world. As such, you should anticipate they will pick up how to use yours.

Your spouse may never comprehend your love language or recognize and encourage your aspirations. Indeed, they can react negatively and cynically if you share your goals and aspirations with them. You cannot expect to be the best friend you would want by your side—

someone who is kind, compassionate, considerate, understanding, and supportive of your aspirations, hopes, and views.

What, then, do you do? When you decide to stay with your narcissistic partner, how do you satisfy these needs? Change your mindset and anticipate that your wants will be satisfied by devoted family members or friends elsewhere. Seek support from your stable social circles who value your goals and aspirations. Have a support system, and work on building wholesome relationships. Put your emotional resources into those who inspire and motivate you to pursue your aspirations. They will be your rock when your marriage or love connection goes south.

Something happens when you change your mindset and stop expecting to feel the emotional pull you so desperately want. You gave up trying to be in charge of a lot of things in the relationship. You become more self-reliant. You gain sufficientity. And then, you may start a journey of self-love, which is a wonderful thing to go through, particularly if your partner makes you feel worthless and unlovable.

You'll find that your frustrations gradually fade when you adjust your expectations. You are no longer demanding. You thus stop feeling anxious or, more crucially, let down. When you are with a narcissist, one of the main emotions you experience is disappointment. You have great expectations every time, but suddenly, a flood of disappointment hits.

But when you become familiar with your partner's narcissistic behavior patterns, you can predict when the fuse will go off and when a fight is about to break out. You'll even be able to predict when the denial and gaslighting will occur. You can lessen your disappointment by being aware of what to expect. Your chances of being let down by your spouse or partner are higher the less you expect and presume from them.

The Value of Limitations

When we think about relationships, we frequently picture a secure refuge. You want your partner to be your haven, somewhere you can go, let all your emotions out, and be met with understanding and sincere compassion. However, if you are with a narcissist, this is not the case. They will turn your moments of susceptibility and weakness into tools of attack. They will use those opportunities to humiliate, dehumanize, and ridicule you.

Which means you have just one option left: set limits. How is it possible to establish limits? Put yourself first. You cannot feed into the narcissist's self-centeredness and prioritize his needs and wants since he is already self-centered. Rather, prioritize your needs. Ensure your mental and emotional well-being. Plan therapy sessions, visit the gym, and engage in favorite activities. Direct your attention towards the pursuits and interests that bring you joy and inspiration. Give these items top attention in your weekly and everyday routine.

Reducing the personal information you provide is another crucial aspect of setting boundaries. You keep giving of yourself until you run out of energy, which is one of the main causes of your mental and emotional exhaustion. Save some of that love and attention for yourself, and give it to yourself instead of sacrificing yourself. Give those who adore and value you your love and emotional support.

Even if you know you may be of assistance to your partner, do not let them abuse you. Don't go above and beyond for your partner. Put on emotional armor instead. Don't divulge too much about your feelings. Stay superficial and basic. Will putting all of these responses and habits into practice first be difficult? Indeed. Your hope threads will pull at your heart, especially when your lover seems to understand, so it won't be easy, and you'll give in.

It will be tempting to revert to your compassionate, empathic ways and treat him that way, but eventually, it will backfire. Narcissists will always revert to their default behaviors, which include denial, gaslighting, dehumanization, belittling, shame, and ridicule. Remember that a narcissist's good deeds are typically motivated by a selfish goal. They always consider their demands and are inherently self-centered.

To be prepared, be alert and make an effort to recognize your partner's narcissistic tendencies. Most significantly, you can develop your response skills. Remember that in this kind of interpersonal dynamic, you come first. Regardless of what your partner says or believes, you must take care of yourself and pursue your ambitions. Live for yourself and direct your attention towards the activities and connections that make you happy and healthy.

Be prudent in your approach if you decide to end the marriage or relationship. Divorce from a narcissist can turn sour, violent, and spiteful. The narcissist will try to ruin you, and if you have children, be prepared for a custody dispute. For you, I have one word: get ready. Get ready on an emotional, mental, and financial level. Ask for legal counsel. Investigate further without informing your partner. If not, you risk their resentment, which adds even more complexity to the process. Put on mental armor and arm yourself well, to put it another way.

You should be aware of everything said above because narcissists frequently marry or date women who don't identify the characteristics their spouse is displaying. You feel inadequate and alone because no one can relate to you, which makes you desperate. You don't know who to ask for help or what else to do because you feel like you're going insane. You can finally put a name on habits that undermine your sense of self, your self-worth, and the depletion of your love reserves when you read this book and feel understood.

How to Handle a Person with a Narcissistic Personality Disorder is covered in Chapter 4.

Having a person with narcissistic personality disorder in your life can be challenging. It may make daily living challenging, if not impossible.

You don't have to give up hope, though. You have options to improve your circumstances and manage your loved one's symptoms more easily. It calls for a strong individual prepared to confront the other person and refuse to back down from their outbursts and deceptive actions. This chapter will outline practical actions you can take to prevent the NPD sufferer from taking over your life.

First and foremost, it is crucial to stop supporting their actions. You must keep in mind that you are under no obligation to comply with the narcissist's requests, particularly if they are immoral or against the law. It may take some time for the person with NPD to cease their maladaptive behavior, but when you put your foot down, it can help them stop because they are accustomed to getting their way.

This implies that initially, they might get angry and yell or exhibit other signs of displeasure.

Now is the perfect time to give up. You don't have to stay if the person seems menacing or is having a tantrum. It is your right to self-defense. Saying no, assuring them that you still care about them, and then turning away are the best courses of action when dealing with someone who has NPD. Refuse to give in to their attempts at manipulation. Be sure to keep the individual and the behavior apart. Tell them that although you care about them and believe they are nice, you cannot grant their request and will not put up with their actions.

You must avoid escalating their rage, too. If you refuse to give in to them, they will likely become angry, but you are not required to join. Remain composed, avoid interacting with them, and leave if they cannot manage their rage. It might be quite challenging to accomplish this. After all, you can be harboring unresolved resentment against the individual attempting to control you. You may be feeling angry and want to vent to them. They will only gain control in the relationship if you give in to their emotions. When you are with them, you should not become furious with them; instead, you should remain composed and either leave the situation or deal with it.

Naturally, the best course of action following this is learning how to manage your rage. You might find it beneficial to attend therapy on your own. After all, anger can be a destructive emotion; if you can't control it, you'll probably end up taking it out on other people or turning it inside on yourself. This is particularly true if you have a close loved one with NPD, such as a spouse, parent, or child. A person close to you may make you feel angry more intensely. This implies that you should take every appropriate action to manage your rage. Discover coping mechanisms for your emotions and practice relaxation. Humor is a way to defuse tension and feelings or engage in physical activity like vigorous exercise. Take whatever action you can to defuse the anger before it overwhelms you and escalates the issues with your narcissistic loved one.

Being willing to talk to your loved one when you both feel calm is another thing you can do to improve the issue. If this individual is receptive to listening, you might encourage them to investigate different viewpoints and open up to others by gently and logically outlining your own. One of the most basic things you can do is this. Ultimately, NPD treatment aims to help the patient realize that they are not the only important person in the world. You can expedite this process by being open to discussing your viewpoint in discussions.

Make sure you are having a conversation that allows for both giving and receiving when you are with someone narcissistic. Talking about themselves is all this individual is willing to talk about; thus, you should end it. Being prepared to defend your interests is the best method to assist someone with NPD in understanding another individual's viewpoint. Assure the NPD person that you will not engage in discussions solely focused on them.

Next, resist the need to feel guilty for the NPD sufferer. When someone with NPD does not get their way, they frequently attempt to place the blame elsewhere in their lives. Additionally, they attempt to place the blame for their maladaptive behavior elsewhere, such as when an abuser claims that the victim is to blame for getting hit. This is one method an NPD person uses guilt to try and control other people and the circumstances they find themselves in.

You must never forget that their actions are not your fault. You don't need to experience guilt. The NPD sufferer could try to make you feel bad about yourself if you speak up for yourself. Avoid this. They have found success with this tactic in the past. They will be compelled to alter their conduct if their current tactic fails and they cannot get your desired response. For an individual with NPD, behavioral change occurs in this way. It may not happen in a single day since it can be gradual. But if you are persistent, it will happen with time and patience.

And lastly, NEVER apologize. You also do not need to apologize to them because you have no justification for feeling bad about their actions. You don't need to express regret to someone or for someone who mistreats others. Do not hold yourself accountable for them since you are not the cause of their actions, and you are not accountable for them.

It's also critical to recognize some behaviors that are inappropriate to exhibit when interacting with an individual who has NPD. First off, don't hold the individual responsible for their actions. It is one thing to identify the issues and another to assign blame. Don't try to make them feel guilty. This will backfire and make the victim even more defensive, which could result in more behaviors. Don't threaten to leave them after that. This is crucial if you are a spouse or other close relative. Ensure they know they are taken care of rather than putting them in danger. Their conduct may worsen rather than improve if they sense that they will be forsaken. Third, avoid making fun of the NPD sufferer. Don't criticize them or speak poorly of them to others.

Even though things can be challenging, the NPD sufferer must believe they can trust you. You won't be able to assist this person if you can't build trust with them.

To protect yourself and to assist the NPD sufferer, heed this advice. Although you must want to support them, you shouldn't put up with their unpredictable actions. In addition to ensuring that your actions benefit them, you also need to protect yourself. Both of these things are possible if you adhere to the advice in this chapter.

The NPD sufferer will have options about what to do next in the upcoming chapter.

Accepting Your Vulnerability

The Power of Being Vulnerable

One of the most effective strategies for developing real connections and conquering narcissistic tendencies is to embrace vulnerability. Despite the popular belief that vulnerability is a sign of weakness, relationships can be strengthened when people are honest and open about their vulnerabilities. This is because it fosters an environment of mutual understanding, authenticity, and trust.

In order to communicate effectively, one must be honest about one's worries, insecurities, and strengths. People invite stronger connections with others when they let themselves be vulnerable. This reciprocal vulnerability serves as a bridge to strengthen the sense of respect and empathy.

Humility, or recognizing that everyone has flaws and vulnerabilities, also involves vulnerability. In order to overcome narcissism, where an emphasis on superiority can obstruct sincere interactions, humility is essential. People who embrace vulnerability show they are open to learning from their experiences, listening to others, and changing their viewpoints.

Moreover, expressing regret and offering apologies need vulnerability. A certain amount of vulnerability is needed when someone admits their errors and displays regret. This technique emphasizes reciprocal respect and accountability, which helps with personal growth and fortifies relationships.

Vulnerability's strength essentially comes from its capacity to strengthen bonds, encourage empathy, encourage humility, and advance the general development of people and their relationships. It is a crucial step on the path to real, meaningful friendships that go beyond the confines of narcissistic tendencies.

Getting Rid of the Rejection Fear

It takes a transformative journey of self-compassion, resilience development, and challenging negative ideas to overcome the fear of rejection. This dread, frequently motivated by a need for approval from others and a fear of not being accepted or appreciated by them, can be very difficult to overcome. The following are essential ideas to get over your fear of rejection:

Disprove Negative Thoughts:

Determine which unfavorable beliefs underlie the fear of rejection and address them. These opinions are frequently predicated on presumptions and prior encounters. Reconsider them, understanding that being rejected does not define who you are.

Develop a Compassionate Self:

Treat yourself with kindness. Recognize that being rejected does not correspond to being unworthy or unlovable. Treat yourself with the same compassion and understanding that you would extend to a friend experiencing comparable anxiety to cultivate self-compassion.

Put Internal Validation First:

Turn your attention from obtaining approval from others to developing validation from within. Recognize your value independent of other people's perspectives. Having a strong sense of self-worth helps one become less reliant on approval from others.

Have Reasonable Expectations: It's important to realize that not every encounter will result in acceptance, and that's perfectly acceptable. Have reasonable expectations for social interactions and understand that rejection doesn't make you less valuable; it's a normal part of life.

Take Advice from Rejections:

Consider rejection a chance to improve rather than a sign of failure. Consider the event, note any trends or opportunities for growth, and utilize it as a springboard for your growth.

Develop Your Resilience

Build resiliency by creating coping strategies to overcome rejection. This may be doing things you enjoy, asking friends for help, or using mindfulness techniques to maintain awareness and attention.

Step Outside Your Comfort Zone: Make an effort to put yourself in circumstances that will make you fear rejection. You develop resilience and desensitize yourself to the imagined possibility of rejection by stepping outside your comfort zone. Appreciate your little progress along the way.

Honor Your Advantages:

Pay attention to your achievements and strong points. Honor the characteristics that set you apart and add value to the world. A positive self-image strengthens one's sense of value and reduces the fear of rejection.

Close friends about your worries. Talking to someone about your worries might help you overcome your fear of rejection by offering helpful insight, motivation, and support.

Engage in Mindfulness Practices: Mindfulness practices, such as deep breathing and being present at the moment, can assist in reducing anxiety associated with rejection anxiety. Being mindful encourages serenity and keeps racing thoughts from getting out of control.

It takes time to overcome the fear of rejection and entails developing self-compassion, emotional resilience, and altered mental habits. People can overcome the limitations of this fear and create stronger, more satisfying relationships with others and themselves by accepting rejection as a normal part of life, learning from mistakes, and concentrating on internal validation.

By using this tactic, you stop them from stealing your focus and energy.

Imagine how you would engage with a coworker or acquaintance you are not very close to: you would be kind, nice, and respectful, but you would also be emotionally cold and dull, like a grey rock.

Recall that grey rocking is an interim tactic, a way to deal with narcissists without letting your feelings get in the way.

Handling A Self-Centered Mother-in-Law

She is disparaging you in front of your husband. She is ruining family get-togethers. You have repeatedly warned her not to give your kids candy, yet she is still doing it.

How do you handle it? It's really easy. Whenever you see her in front of the family, you treat her gracefully and elegantly. Although you are polite and pleasant, you never discuss with her.

Never divulge to her any private information about you or your partner. To ensure that she has nothing on you and cannot mistreat you, limit your responses to one word or sentence.

How does that appear in daily life? Perhaps she will ask you:

"How is your work progressing?"

What you say in answer is:

"Everything is going great. I appreciate you asking.

So, if she attempts to start something along these lines:

"Well, what about that girl who didn't like you at work?"

Once more, you grey rock with something akin to:

"At work, I get along with everyone. But I appreciate your care.

The egotistical mother-in-law enjoys making fun of you publicly to make you feel better. She makes you look bad in front of your husband or kids. In a devious power ploy, she will also do it privately to establish her dominance over you and demonstrate "who's boss" in the family.

There are a tonne of grey rock responses you might have when this occurs. You may state:

"I wonder what you were trying to say when you commented."

"Right now, that is not the place or time to discuss that."

"If we could switch the topic, that would be appreciated."

"I apologize if you feel that way."

"I won't respond to that comment because I find it offensive."

That's how you saw what happened. I have a different perspective on things.

Breaking Free from Negative Feelings

Emotions such as anger, envy, and jealousy can become ingrained in your life and lead to serious issues. It's critical to acknowledge their presence and take action to eliminate them. Being free of these kinds of feelings is a process that takes time. You must dedicate yourself to long-term labor and upkeep even after free.

Negative feelings are strong; if you don't control them, they can easily become habits. For instance, if you react angrily to criticism all the time, eventually, this pattern will make you feel that way whenever you receive criticism. Your relationships, job, and other aspects of your life may begin to suffer.

Give Up Justification

Stopping yourself from rationalizing your bad feelings is the first step. If you constantly become upset, own up to the reason and quit blaming others. *Anger* is a strong feeling that may easily turn into a habit. You can begin to reassess why you feel this way so that you can alter it as soon as you acknowledge that this behavior is troublesome and that it is not good.

Give Up Making Excuses

You are telling yourself that you have no control over unpleasant feelings when you rationalize them away, whether they are directed at you or someone else. This is untrue since you always have a choice in responding to a given circumstance. You will never own up to your mistakes if you keep finding reasons not to do what you did. People may eventually begin to withdraw from your life because they will not want to be around someone who cannot own up to their mistakes or faults.

Accept Responsibility

When you commit to stopping your justifications, you can begin accepting some accountability for your actions in different circumstances. First, deprive your negative feelings of their potency. You'll discover they can't control you if you accept responsibility. Making the appropriate decisions and responses will inevitably begin to come more easily.

Avoid Overanalyzing What Other People Think of You

Although you are ultimately responsible for controlling your emotions, outside circumstances may make it more difficult. What other people think of you is one of the most important external influences. This is particularly valid if the person criticizing you is very outspoken. Narcissists frequently attempt to manipulate you by acting in this way.

It is in human nature to want to be liked and wanted. It's human nature to respond negatively to remarks made about you by someone you respect or care about. Instead, you should listen to what they say before deciding whether or not to believe it. Did your boss, for instance, scream at you for a tiny mistake you made on a project at work? Think about their yelling. Consider the larger picture. All right, you made a tiny error, but other than that, you finished the project and performed satisfactorily. Keep this in mind, and let the criticism fall off of you.

Give Up Your Negative Habits

Any negative habit you have has the potential to worsen your circumstances. For instance, frequently consuming fast food, smoking, or failing to practice oral hygiene. Spend a moment writing down all of your negative habits. Put them in writing, and they become more recognizable. Can you dedicate a lot of attention to it? Start focusing on one at a time. Your emotions will gain from your efforts to improve your overall well-being.

Shut Down Negative Individuals

Move on from those who are primarily a bad influence in your life. How long you have known them or how close you are makes no difference. Their continuous negativity is not improving your life in any way. You might think about conversing with them if you truly care about them. But not everyone can change, and some people might not choose to. A narcissist, for instance, finds it difficult to just quit acting negatively. It's ingrained in their character. That's why you won't go anywhere by merely chatting to them.

Consider Your Reaction Before Saying Anything

Because they are so strong, negative feelings frequently just come out. On the other hand, practice delaying responding to anything that makes you feel bad for ten seconds. This enables you to collect yourself so that your reaction is situation-appropriate. For instance, you were an hour late for a dinner appointment with a friend. They're angry. Instead of just getting back at them and starting a fight, give it ten counts, then think about why they are angry. It will be simpler to realize that you should apologize and that they did nothing wrong.

Be Appreciative

You should be thankful for the amazing things in your life, even in the darkest circumstances. It helps to lessen the bad emotions when you focus on them rather than the negative. You can think about maintaining a journal and then spend a few minutes at the end of each day listing all the positive things that happened. The good things in your life will eventually begin to organically outweigh the bad.

Give Up Saying "I Can't"

You will gradually believe you cannot do something if you repeatedly tell yourself. It's said that this is a self-fulfilling prophecy. Give yourself a break and quit restricting yourself to what is comfortable and simple. You automatically drive out the negative emotions as you push yourself and realize how many things you are good at. This puts you in a more positive frame of mind.

Let It Go: If everything could be controlled, life would be much easier, but that's unrealistic. Recognize and let go of things you cannot control when you encounter them. As an illustration, not everyone will like you, and occasionally, a loved one may become enraged with you over an incident that was not your fault. Don't push the matter further. Give it a chance, and things will come together in the end.

Simpler actions can be taken daily to assist you in overcoming unpleasant feelings and improve your general well-being. Though you don't have to do them all daily, you should think about them and apply them to your schedule when it makes sense. Among them are:

Take action and resist letting the bad things simply become a part of your life.

Cry it out when things are difficult because it can help you feel less stressed.

For a short while, scream as loudly as possible, which balances out negative feelings.

Get some sleep; when you're not weary, dealing with stress and bad feelings is simpler.

Try to stay upbeat and see the bright side of things regardless of what occurs.

Set aside time to laugh every day since laughing makes it impossible to feel bad. Find a trusted person who cares about you and contact them for support.

Examine a different angle to see if it could help you address an issue more effectively.

You can forgive yourself for setbacks if you acknowledge them and don't let them fully derail you.

Own your emotions; when you feel bad, acknowledge it, think about why you're feeling it, and then let go of it.

Before you go to bed every night, write about your day or the experience you just had. This helps you put the bad things behind you and start over the next day.

The Drug Of The Narcissist

Like a junkie, the narcissist is constantly in need of his drug. This is what lends his life significance or validates his existence. The narcissist initially fabricates his image or fake self in order to satisfy his needs. He created this fictional character to represent the kind of guy he wishes he could be but knows he is not. In order to get the reactions he wants, he maintains this façade as a sort of bait. What fuels his ego is the reaction to this constructed image. The narcissist is always in need of what is known as the "narcissistic supply."

Self-centered Supply

He is comparable to a vampire in that he needs a constant supply of love, respect, approval, assistance, and support rather than blood. He believes that without the narcissistic supply, life has no purpose. He will continue to accept criticism with gratitude. The narcissist values positive or negative attention. The narcissist, in contrast to a normal individual, is never content and only gets minimal amounts of reinforcement and acceptance. Because it's his drug, he needs more. He has an insatiable hunger for this supply and will stop at nothing to get his hands on it. His partner, girlfriend, friends, coworkers, or even strangers could give it to him. A person is not necessarily the source. His profession, gift, pet, or belongings might also satisfy his need for narcissistic supply.

Main Source of Narcissistic Supply

This is a reference to the narcissist's random access to a general supply of attention. Public resources like reputation, renown, and recognition may be available. It could also be something said in private, such as an attack or a compliment. If the narcissist's major source is the enormous ocean, his yearning would be for water.

Secondary Source of Narcissism

This is a reference to the consistent supply that the narcissist knows will be available. Returning to the water analogy, the water bottles he stores in his refrigerator would represent his secondary supply if the wide ocean serves as his primary source. The narcissist sees to it that he keeps supplies in a convenient location so he may access them anytime he needs them. He gets it from things or people that he interacts with frequently, such as his spouse, students, and coworkers.

The narcissist uses the secondary supply to maintain his false self because he is highly image-conscious. He typically wants to come across as prosperous, steady, normal, powerful, and even mysterious.

The Injury of the Narcissist

By now, it should be clear that the narcissist utilizes his supply to satisfy the emptiness that he perceives as being so real. He's good as long as he gets his supply. However, what occurs if the supply is interrupted? The narcissist will have withdrawal symptoms when confronted with the bottomless hole within of him, just like a drug addict would if their fix were taken away. He'll become confused and irritated over it. It might potentially trigger a psychotic episode. The narcissist finds it unable to acknowledge or accept his own needs. When his ego is injured, he experiences narcissistic harm. The narcissist's god complex takes control as he still cannot believe that his painstakingly constructed false image is flawed, and he swears to get revenge on whoever is holding back his supply. The narcissist deludes himself into thinking that he is hurt.

The Fury of the Narcissist

It is not the narcissist's desire to identify as a victim. However, he feels betrayed since the narcissistic supply is being stopped. The narcissist's outrage stems from his frustration at having his valuable supply cut off. His response would be to avenge the wrongdoer or strike back, then return right away to resuming his narcissistic feed. His fury might vary from being non-violent to becoming physical. It could be poisonous, violent, or passive-aggressive. The narcissist believes that his angry outburst is entirely justified because he has been abused. However, his anger appears unjustified to the average person as a response to a sequence of neutral circumstances.

How to Get Away

You can't move forward with success as long as you're still under the narcissist's influence. Because of this, you must end your relationship with them before you can go forward in anything you do.

It will be difficult for you to leave your spouse because you have been together for a long time and may even have children together.

You can, however, effectively quit the person if you follow the appropriate advice.

These are a few different pieces of advice to assist you in safely leaving an abusive relationship.

Give Them Another Chance.

An abusive narcissist will attempt to entice you back to them after you leave, at which point they will discard you. A narcissist's primary goal is to ensure that you are always the one at fault.

When things aren't done according to their terms, they find a method to get things done the other way around. The narcissist will put in the work and beg you, telling you how sorry they are if they are not yet ready to go.

Try not to give them another opportunity to control you for you to go. They will start appealing, pleading with you, and expressing their regret, pleading with you to return.

Never Inform Them That You're Leaving

Notifying the narcissist that you're ending the relationship is not necessary. This is due to the possibility that it will prime them to begin love bombing you in an attempt to keep you in the marriage. They even have the power to threaten their own lives in an attempt to keep you trapped.

Possess Some Extra Money

When considering leaving, ensure you have enough money to start your new life. In order to avoid having to return to the person who supports you when the time comes to part ways, start saving money well in advance.

You must act in secret if your partner is abusing you in order to prevent them from cutting you off completely.

Report the mistreatment

Reporting the abuse is imperative, even if you cannot involve the police in the issue. When you enter, explain what has been occurring to you and, if applicable, display any apparent injuries.

You will have documentation from your recorded statement when you want to present your case later.

Exit from Every Device

You should be sure to change the passwords on any devices you share with your partners if you plan to stay logged in so they can't follow you. Reset all of your login information and make new ones.

Hence, compile a list of all the websites you have visited, spent your credit card, and any auto-fills you have ever had, and then remove them all.

Ensuring you aren't being tracked comes next when you log off the gadgets. Get rid of the phone if you can, then replace it with a functional one.

Don't Let the Flattery Sway You

A narcissist will attempt to stop you from leaving by flattery or any other tactic. The intention is to create an atmosphere in which you feel compelled to depart.

The narcissist will make an effort to surpass your expectations in several ways, such as purchasing your presents and providing you with the attention you've always craved.

Reestablish Contact With Friends and Family

In order to focus on you and keep you away from the family, an abusive narcissist will seek to. Some people who used to be close to you may not have been around you, or you may have ignored them. Reestablishing contact with them is crucial, though, so that they can help you heal.

But when they notice you, you must overcome your shyness and embarrassment. If you need to apologize, swallow your pride and do it.

You'll discover how many people had attempted to assist you but were unable to when you get in touch with them again. Though unsure where to begin or what to do, they may have attempted to assist.

Clear the Decks

Now is the moment to determine who is detrimental to your cause and remove them. You'll make your choice, but not everyone will accept it with the understanding you hope for. They'll act like they're the greatest people in the world while pointing fingers at you.

This is your chance to remove some people from your life, particularly those detrimental to your objectives.

Handling the Narcissist in the Workplace: Useful Communication Strategies

The deceptive and self-centered actions of a narcissist can have a detrimental effect on the culture of the workplace and team relationships. Nonetheless, there are useful communication strategies that can support a more positive and cooperative work atmosphere while managing relationships with narcissists.

Identifying the symptoms of pathological narcissism is the first step towards managing a narcissist at work. Learn about the characteristics of narcissism, which include an ongoing desire for approval. Knowing these characteristics will enable you to tackle the narcissist's behavior more thoughtfully and with greater understanding.

Remain composed and calm.

Being cool and collected is crucial when dealing with narcissists. Narcissists may try to exploit your weaknesses since they are skilled at evoking strong emotions in others. Refrain from engaging in disputes or disagreements, and be aware of your feelings. You may lessen the likelihood that the narcissist will emotionally manipulate you and make you react by remaining composed.

Be Confident and Clear in Your Expressions

It's imperative to communicate with narcissists forcefully. Communicate clearly and concisely, stating your demands and ideas in an authoritative yet kind manner. Refrain from being unclear or obedient since the narcissist could exploit your ambiguity. Acquire the ability to defend your beliefs and boundaries without succumbing to their deceptive strategies.

Put the facts and objective data first.

Information manipulation and truth distortion are common traits of narcissists. Try to keep your conversation with a narcissist grounded in reality and unbiased information. Refrain from engaging in disputes that stem from feelings or arbitrary interpretations. Presenting hard facts and impartial data can lessen the likelihood that the narcissist will distort reality to suit them.

Establish Discreet and Uniform Boundaries

Narcissists have a propensity to cross lines and take advantage of their connections. Establish firm limits on the behavior of the narcissist, both in terms of what you will and won't accept. When imposing boundaries, maintain your composure and firmness. It can take a few instances of assertiveness before the narcissist realizes they can't go beyond your boundaries. In a meeting, for example, if the narcissist frequently dominates the talk, you could say, "I appreciate your input, but I'd also like the opportunity to share my ideas."

Refrain from Taking Things Personally

Selfish behavior and self-centeredbehavior are common traits of narcissists. While engaging with a narcissist, keep in mind that their actions are frequently the consequence of their personality condition rather than something you've done. Refrain from taking things personally or allowing them to do you harm.

Rather, concentrate on preserving equilibrium and safeguarding your psychological welfare.

Seek Assistance and Face Leadership

Seek help from coworkers, friends, or family if dealings with the narcissist become extremely harmful or complex. You can get emotional support and release pent-up anger by talking to someone you trust. If the narcissist's behaviors are negatively affecting your health or the productivity of your team, you should think about speaking with the HR department or the company's leadership. Giving details regarding the circumstance can guarantee that pathological narcissism is dealt with properly.

Preserve Your Work-Life Harmony

Keeping a work-life balance is crucial since dealing with narcissists at work may be exhausting. It's important to remember to take time for oneself and partake in rejuvenating and relaxing activities. Maintaining a healthy work-life balance can safeguard your mental health and help you cope with the stress brought on by your contact with the narcissist.

Think About Getting Expert Assistance

If you find that dealing with the narcissist is difficult or harmful to your emotional health, you might want to think about getting help from a psychologist or psychotherapist. You can improve your mental wellbeing at work and deal with the narcissist by developing targeted methods with the assistance of a specialist.

Meanwhile, try these powerful and tried-and-true sentences to defuse your egotistical coworker:

"I appreciate your viewpoints, but I would also like to share my ideas about this project."

"I'm glad you succeeded with that project, but I would ask that you not take full credit for it, as the team worked hard together."

"I would be open to collaborating with you to find a solution to this issue, but please avoid making disparaging or belittling comments about my ideas."

"I understand you're busy, but I would appreciate it if you could find a moment to listen to my concerns about our project."

"I understand you feel confident about your approach, but I would appreciate you considering the perspectives of the rest of the team as well."

"Thank you for your feedback, but I would prefer to receive constructive criticism that helps me improve, rather than dismissive comments."

"I am aware of my strengths and skills, so I would prefer if you didn't question my ability to do my job."

"I'm sorry if you got the impression that I'm showing off, but I'm simply trying to share my experiences for the benefit of the project."

"I don't think it's necessary to speak negatively about other team members. Let's focus on how we can collaborate effectively."

"I would like our work environment to be more positive and constructive. I hope we can resolve our differences and work as a united team."

Remember to be assertive while remaining composed and respectful of your egotistical coworker. Instead of getting sucked into the toxic dynamics the narcissist creates, try to remain detached and focused on the subjects at hand. You might be able to control your colleague's behavior and make the workplace better with the appropriate attitude and communication.

I am aware that dealing with narcissists effectively manages the dynamics and fosters a positive work atmosphere by using the appropriate communication skills. When dealing with a narcissist, maintaining your cool, communicating assertively and clearly, and establishing clear limits are crucial skills. Remind yourself not to take their actions personally and ask for help when needed. Maintaining a more upbeat and cooperative work environment can be achieved by skillfully handling encounters with narcissists, which will boost the team's well-being as a whole.

You see, the daughter of a narcissistic mother has never had someone who could relate to her for most of her life. She would benefit from having a positive female role model to aspire to. That woman may be her buddy's mother, her aunt, a family friend, a coworker, a teacher, or any number of others.

It will support her in thriving for the years, not just getting through this predicament. It is a much-needed adjustment to have someone who understands her suffering, and it can aid in the grieving process.

Remain free from obstacles, both real and imagined.

Don't get stuck—take this counsel seriously.

Avoid being cooped up in the house all day. That will just make you feel worse. Avoid being mired in your sentiments of resentment and irritation. Release them. Additionally, let yourself out the door.

Step outside. Visit a new location. Try a novel approach.

Consult your physician. Make an appointment with your therapist right now. Take up a new pastime. Increasing the number of new experiences in your life will assist you in rediscovering the purpose that you could have missed while living alone with your narcissistic parent.

It would be quite beneficial for you to have a solid support network throughout this period. Family and friends are the ideal people to light a fire under you if it appears you're getting stuck, but they will also give you space when needed. Inform them of your desire to explore new experiences, your search for a therapist, or even your desire not to go more than X days without leaving your home. They will assist you in any way they can, even if it involves "kidnapping" you to have lunch at the new deli near Grandma's house (just as my brother did at the behest of my paternal grandma).

Plan and manage your time.

Accept that time and money are similar. It's a kind of mental and emotional money. Like money, time is something that never goes away. You never run out of money because you will eventually make more, even if you lose some.

With time, the same holds. You can use it prudently right now or hold onto it for an unspecified future day. Even if you won't be here forever, you can always find time to enjoy every day. Don't waste it, and quit thinking about the past.

Make something worthwhile out of your experiences.

Every encounter in life serves as a teaching opportunity. Rather than dwelling on the anguish and suffering caused by your narcissistic mother, consider finding lessons to be learned from her.

Try to see a terrible incident from a different angle whenever it resurfaces in your memory. Look for something that teaches you something. Approach it as you would a book. Yes, you have reviewed it numerous times. However, there are more religious themes that you can learn from, just like any book.

Salute life!

If you are forced to stay fixated on the suffering and loss you went through with your narcissistic mother, it is a terrible injustice. You cannot heal or move on while you remain in that state.

As an alternative, you could rejoice in your newfound ability to live your own life. Now that the past has passed, it is time to move on. It was once remarked that the only thing we can do about the past is accept it. Since we cannot foretell the future, it is not entirely ours. This is the one moment that you can influence.

My current therapist has a copy of a Bil Keane cartoon strip from 1994 called "The Family Circus" stuck to the back of her laptop. The caption underneath the graphic says, "Today is a GIFT, but tomorrow is a mystery." Yesterday is the past. That's why it's called the present. This may sound corny, but it helps me remember to embrace the current moment whenever I wonder why I wasn't good enough or returning to how my mother treated me.

This is all you know, so you have to live in the now. Nobody is holding the strings now. Now that you are free, your whole life is waiting to be experienced by you and you alone.

Strategies For Handling A Narcissistic Parent

The real issue with narcissistic parents is that they don't only exhibit selective narcissism. Many people will criticize their parents for being clingy, needy, or embarrassed during family gatherings. But, narcissistic parents go well beyond what is considered appropriate for awkward and irritating parenting to the point where it seriously harms their child's emotional growth. One of the worst parenting blunders committed by narcissistic parents is their self-centeredness.

When you grow up around narcissists and get tired of their mind games, one of the main questions you ask yourself is how you would handle them now that you are an adult. We're going to examine a few different scenarios, but they're all generally supportive of the notion of escaping the cruel and uncaring grasp of the narcissistic parent.

We will begin by reviewing what we've already covered: the vital need to acknowledge that your parents are fallible. Admitting that there was an issue and that, regrettably, you were not above the abhorrent and repulsive chances of the cosmos is one of the most difficult aspects of moving on from abuse in general. Anyone can experience it, and, regrettably, you could as well.

I am going to suggest something completely unimaginable to you. Maybe you don't have to stay in touch with your parents. The last fifty years, in particular, have seen a slight shift in how society views parent-child interactions. One thing that has changed is the increased awareness of physical, emotional, and mental abuse. These things that were generally accepted as unquestionable or as a harsh fact of life that wasn't discussed would later be perceived as powerfully detrimental factors. The violent or abusive undertones seen in family structures are no longer acceptable in society.

In addition, people now consider leaving one's parents behind as a viable alternative in the event of abuse. Some cultures, on the other hand, reject this idea since they still value family relationships above all else and, in the end, you should have the utmost respect for your parents, whether or not they deserve it.

Thankfully, reality doesn't always support this theory, and in the current environment, ending contact with abusive parents is beginning to be recognized as a more sensible choice. Every age is coming around to accepting afflicted people's decision to break off contact with their abusive or narcissistic parents, even if it will still garner you strange stares.

Thus, essentially, the first thing you should do to deal with narcissistic parents is to give them as little influence as possible. Since this is generally the best course of action, much of this section will concentrate on it. The fact is, narcissism is really about how one person asserts power over another and compels that other to support their extremely flimsy ego and self-image. As such, it is not unusual for narcissistic parents to use all methods at their disposal to maintain control over you. Because of this, you must take these off as soon as possible because you should put up a plan if you haven't already. If your narcissistic parents are still your primary caregivers, secretly arrange your move out of their house. You probably have some options at your disposal. For instance, if you're a college student, you can probably live on campus and receive some financial assistance from the institution. Moreover, you could even be able to borrow money in order to improve your quality of life.

The second thing you should think about is what, if anything, you actively and presently depend on them for. Are they, in one way or another, your lifeline? Do they now take care of payments for your phone bill and auto insurance? If so, you should include these items in your plan. Calculate how much it will cost to complete these tasks independently, then add that amount to the total cost of living when evaluating rent pricing.

Unfortunately, your parents will stop your attempts to move out if these kinds of things are present. You should prepare for the moment when they do just that, as they will still threaten to cut them off. You need to include these demands in your plan if they've already moved out or you're away for college and they're still attempting to exert undue control over your life. Examples of such demands include not letting you date while in college, threatening to stop paying your car payments, refusing to assist you with your loan payments, or turning off your phone.

The first thing you'll need to do is find employment if you don't already have one. Sadly, narcissistic parents frequently forbid their kids from working since it gives them a sense of independence and reduces their dependence on the narcissistic parent. As a result, you might have to couch surf with friends until you accumulate enough cash to support yourself. If this occurs, attempt to budget for these because you can find yourself without a phone or insurance for a few months. If you don't have insurance, stay away from driving and plan to use the public transportation system in your area, if available, or try to get rides from friends and coworkers to and from your obligations.

In reality, all you're attempting to do is lessen any potential grip they may have over you to remove that source of power. The truth is that if you're dealing with narcissistic parents, there's very little likelihood that they will ever realize that their actions are narcissistic. This might be the most challenging part of the process. It's likely that they will never even possess the necessary self-awareness to do so. This puts you in a difficult situation that you never really asked for. Either you try to minimize your interactions with your parents and try to cut down on your overall amount of time spent with them, complete healing, or you have to keep talking to them and run the risk of always having that toxic and narcissistic person in your life.

Ultimately, it's regrettable, but you will probably need to break up with them or drastically reduce your contact with them if you truly want to be given the chance to develop as a person and begin healing from some of the trauma that has resulted from growing up with narcissists.

Sadly, they are unable to keep up good relationships because they simply do not want to. Wishing away your problems won't solve this one. Furthermore, it won't work out for you no matter how hard you try to persuade them to change their behavior or work through the reasons behind their actions. In the best-case scenario, they trick you into believing that they will change to slowly revert to their previous state as if nothing had ever happened.

That's not true, though. If your parents are narcissists, their best chance is that they will be able to examine what goes on and what drives it within. Progress might be gained if they truly understand you and are prepared to put you above themselves. But you can't count on this to happen.

Purposeful distortion of one's ideas.

A narcissist sees your unique thoughts, emotions, and experiences as personal shortcomings. Narcissists will recount your experiences in order to make your beliefs and ideas appear ludicrous. A narcissist might say something like, "So you think you're perfect then?" in response to you discussing a friend who is acting toxically crazy toward you. They'll take what you tell them and turn it around to paint you negatively. This gives them the ability to discredit your thoughts and feelings about inappropriate behavior, which they can then use to incite guilt in you if you attempt to set limits with them. This manipulation technique is known as "mind-reading" from a psychological perspective and is a type of cognitive distortion or diversion. When you say something, narcissists will draw assumptions without pausing to properly assess the circumstances. They will put words in your mouth to give the impression that you have a bizarre viewpoint, so they may use it against you later.

Pretending to be innocent

Narcissists may give you a false sense of security, so they may better inflict their brutality on you. They could try to draw you into a pointless argument to make you feel foolish and unwelcome. A straightforward argument can quickly escalate into a scenario in which the narcissist is attempting to undermine you and destroy your sense of worth. Narcissists are likely aware of your fears, so they know just how to undermine your self-worth or bring up hurtful subjects. They provoke you because they know you. Their fake, innocent statements will lead you to feel that they didn't mean to hurt you, but that doesn't mean it's not wrong. If you fall for it and get upset at their behavior, they may back off and say, "I didn't mean to upset you!" Knowing when one is being baited is very helpful for victims. In this manner, you can completely avoid participating in their poisonous dialogue.

Disgrace

Narcissists frequently resort to shame when they believe their sense of self is being questioned. The purpose of shame is to undermine the victim's sense of self-worth. The narcissists will blame their victim for anything, even if it is something they are proud of, like an accomplishment, in an attempt to suppress their pride. Because narcissists like taking advantage of your vulnerabilities, they will shame you for pretty much anything in your past in an attempt to relive the trauma. They believe that picking at an existing wound is the most effective approach to cause harm to their victims.

avoiding responsibility

Because narcissists are never willing to take responsibility for anything, they will deliberately reroute and divert conversations to their advantage. Suppose you question your narcissistic mother about their inattentive parenting, for example. In that case, she may bring up earlier mistakes you made to shift the topic away from them and toward you. Narcissists employ this diversion approach to sabotage talks that might question their status quo or their vision of themselves. It has no boundaries regarding subject or time; it usually begins with "Well, what about the time when you..." Anything that could jeopardize their appearance will be deflected by blaming someone else and drawing attention elsewhere. Don't allow them to stop you if this occurs to you. Remain focused on the facts, and don't let your attention wander.

proactivedefense

A narcissist will use this manipulative tactic to try to establish credibility with you by telling you to "trust them" right away because they seem like a "nice guy" or "nice girl," all without offering any supporting proof. Narcissists frequently exaggerate how sympathetic and caring they are. They won't bother trying to earn people's trust by telling them to just "trust" them. Even while they may first appear to have great sympathy or empathy, they will eventually take off the false façade. Sincere lovely people's good traits are evident in their actions and behaviors; thus, they don't need to express them verbally. They understand mutual respect and trust are based on reciprocity rather than repetition.

Defamation, slander, and stalking

A narcissist will attempt to manipulate how other people perceive you if they can't get you to see yourself the way you want. They will pretend to be a saint to make you appear toxic to others. They will publicly malign you to damage your reputation, leaving you without someone to go on for support. To get in contact with them and "expose" you as the "bad person" you are, they might even go so far as to stalk others who are close to you. They are concealing the truth that they are the ones who are terrible by painting you in that role. Narcissists will talk negatively about you to your friends and family behind your back and perhaps even in front of you. They'll fabricate tales to paint you negatively, playing the victim and saying you're scared they will ruin THEIR reputation.

Broad generalizations

We often assume narcissists to be brilliant individuals. However, this isn't the case. Indeed, many of them lack even a modicum of intellectual strength. Despite the various viewpoints you may have explained, they make generalizations or sweeping remarks that ignore your argument rather than take a different stance. In order to uphold their standing and minimize any accomplishments or experiences you might be proud of, their generalizations frequently invalidate many of the experiences you could be sharing with them. For example, charges of sexual harassment made against well-known individuals or popular public figures are frequently met with retaliation that claims fraudulent reports of sexual harassment occur frequently. Although those DO occur, they are extremely uncommon, and this statement does not acknowledge the accused person's acts. Relationships of various kinds, particularly those between a mother and her kid, might experience these things. For example, they frequently respond with a generalization like "you're just too sensitive" or "you are never satisfied" in response to criticism of their narcissistic behavior or a negative action they've taken instead of discussing the specific problems at hand. While it's likely that your narcissistic mother is the one who acts cruelly and insensitively the majority of the time, it's also possible that you are sensitive at times.

Making hurtful remarks while posing as humorous

Narcissists frequently make "jokes" about you. Their insults are typically disguised as "just jokes" so they can keep up their good image and escape having to say awful things to you. They tell you you lack humor or don't appreciate their jokes when you get upset about their hurtful comments. This is simply another method that they will mislead you and lead you to believe that they are not cruel when, in fact, they are, by gaslighting you into believing that their abusive words and acts are a joke.

Forecasting

Narcissists are frequently unable to accept responsibility for their errors and failings and would stop at nothing to avoid it. We refer to this as projection. Projecting blame onto another individual is a defensive tactic used by narcissists to shift accountability from themselves. They use it to escape responsibility and take ownership of their acts. Narcissists will place the blame for their errors on their victims and expect them to accept responsibility for the narcissist's actions rather than owning up to their shortcomings. This is how people with narcissistic tendencies project their shame onto others. When someone experiences narcissistic abuse, they tend to blame everyone else for their problems. Their ego needs to be nursed while being made to doubt themselves.

Handling A Narcissist

Everybody has a propensity toward narcissism. The majority of people exhibit normal levels of narcissism, although there are different levels of the trait.

But, certain people exhibit incredibly high degrees of narcissistic traits. You start to discover that the traits that drew you in and attracted you to that person are narcissistic traits that irritate you greatly.

This individual could be a narcissistic parent, sibling, or other family member. You can't resist or control certain personality qualities; therefore, you must put up with them. You may know a teacher, employee, coworker, boss, or student who exhibits narcissistic traits.

It doesn't mean that all narcissists are nasty people, even though there are some of them. Certain individuals with elevated narcissistic traits can be charming, enjoyable to be around, and exceptionally skilled in their field. They could be able to guide your group to success in the workplace.

Rather than ignoring them and minimizing your dealings with them, you may decide that the narcissist you are engaged with or dealing with is the kind that can be transformed. In this case, you would prefer to support them while they transform. Some narcissists fit into the "vulnerable" category, and you could worry that they'll suffer harm if you ignore them.

As you've read previously, there are differences among narcissists. The type of person you are engaged with should determine how you handle the one in your life.

A grandiose narcissist thinks highly of himself or herself. They might occasionally be just as good as they claim to be.

A vulnerable narcissist truly conceals a weak inner self behind a self-absorbed façade.

Naturally, both of these kinds could also exhibit other traits associated with Machiavellianism, such as denial of guilt, lack of empathy, and manipulativeness (Whitbourne, 2014).

These are the kinds of personality traits that truly irritate others. They are challenging to deal with because of their hatred and hostility, and they will almost always stand in the way of your success.

Showcasing their superiority and discounting the thoughts and emotions of others.

Falling for the Fantasy and the Reasons Not to - Narcissists have a captivating personality. They simply gleam and entice others into their orbit due to their charismatic nature. They are adept at projecting amazing confidence. Getting sucked into their world can be simple. We believe they will fulfill our need to feel vital and significant. But in the end, it's all fantasy, and it costs money (Smith et al., 2018).

You should understand that narcissists seek admirers rather than partners, and they won't acknowledge or satisfy your demands. For the record, the admirer must exhibit obedience. A person with NPD sees you exclusively as someone who can stroke their voracious ego by telling them how amazing they are. You don't matter, nor do your desires or sentiments.

See how people with narcissistic personality disorder manipulate, deceive, treat others disrespectfully, and injure others. Since you are the closest person to them, if they treat others badly, they will also treat you, perhaps even worse.

Never even consider that you are unique and won't receive the same treatment. You will receive the same treatment as everyone else; you are not unique or personally identifiable.

Concentrate on what you want to do for yourself; concentrate on yourself. You should take this route to improve your talent or make changes in your life. Rather than existing in another person's dream, create your reality.

Take off your rose-colored glasses and view the narcissists in your life for what they truly are. Don't try to make them into someone you want them to be. It is not acceptable to downplay or justify their negative actions or the pain they are causing you. Live not in denial.

A narcissist is not adaptable. They view it as a sign of weakness and prefer to come out stronger than others. The true shift must occur when you ask yourself if you want to continue being this way forever or if you want to make the adjustments necessary to save your own life (Smith et al., 2018).

Establish Firm and Healthy Boundaries: The foundation sentiments and consideration for them. On the other hand, if you are close to someone who has NPD, they are unable to feel the same way in relationships. It's not that they can't reciprocate; it's just that they're unwilling. They cannot see, hear, or recognize you. You are an individual who exists independently of your needs and wants. It doesn't fit with your requirements, wants, or feelings. Having stated that narcissists frequently cross other people's boundaries. They not only cross boundaries but also act with complete entitlement and a lack of empathy.

Narcissists don't believe it is impolite or intrusive to take items from you without even asking permission, read your mail and texts, show up at your house without permission, steal your ideas and pretend you came up with them, listen in on conversations without asking permission, or offer unwanted advice or opinions. Certain narcissists may believe they are your brain and can control your thoughts and emotions.

Create a plan: It will be difficult to maintain control if you have boundaries and have enabled others to cross them. Thinking through your objectives and potential obstacles will help you set more rigid boundaries.

In order to create your strategy, you must first decide what changes are most essential to you and what you expect to achieve. Has there ever been a solution for the narcissist that genuinely worked? Is there anything that was unsuccessful? If you start doubting the distribution of authority between the two of you, how will that affect your plan? How will you enforce your new boundaries once you've established them?

Options and creating a sound plan that ought to work for you if you can honestly respond to them.

Chapter 3: Narcissistic Personality Disorder Causes and Symptoms

The precise cause of narcissistic personality disorder (NDP) has not yet been determined by the scientific community, as is typically the case with personality disorders. However, a lot of specialists think that a mix of genes, early life experiences, and psychological factors are the main reasons for this.

Parenting styles and early childhood trauma are two instances of early life experiences linked to the development of NDP. For instance, researchers have found that narcissism and other personality disorders can arise when parents overindulge in their children or focus too much on their skills or attractiveness.

High expectations, trauma or abuse, harsh criticism from parents, and parental neglect are among the variables that might put a youngster at risk for personality disorders like NDP.

We will go into more detail about a few of the primary elements of NDP in this chapter. After completing this, you ought to comprehend the root causes of narcissism more fully:

#: Reluctance To Be a Victim.

One of the main reasons for narcissism, according to licensed clinical psychologist Seth

Meyers, Psy.D., is a strong intolerance to vulnerability.

According to his explanation, narcissism stems from a person's aversion to vulnerability since, even in a relationship, their need to appear flawless prevents them from being able to trust other people. Their fear typically causes the narcissist's inability, or rather reluctance, to trust people that a detailed examination may expose personality flaws.

Meyers goes on to say that narcissism arises when a person is unable to trust people or decides not to since it involves a certain amount of vulnerability. Most narcissists are reluctant to show vulnerability because it conflicts with their false self-image, which is so prevalent in them. Rather, they continue to be extremely watchful against anything they perceive as a challenge to the mental image of their supremacy.

A false internal and external self-image that is driven by fear, particularly the fear of "being found wanting," is typically the root cause of narcissism. In order to safeguard this delicate self-image, those who lean toward narcissism tend to avoid conflict with others for fear that they may discover information that would give them the upper hand.

In addition, most narcissists have a propensity to overcompensate and overdo it in order to preserve a false sense of superiority that prevents vulnerability. For example, a person with a narcissistic disposition may become angry when they feel helpless and exposed. If not, this kind of person is prone to behave in a way that makes them feel in control, even if it means harming others.

Dr. Seth Meyers learned through his clinical work that narcissism arises from the urge to defend a flimsy and false sense of self and ego. He goes on to say that when a person with narcissistic tendencies encounters anything that makes them feel inadequate, they develop an exaggerated, false sense of who they are. The individual then boosts their ego and feels better using this fictitious sense of self-worth.

Dr. Meyers concludes that pathological narcissism arises when someone who feels "deficient" constructs a false, narcissistic inner character rather than reflecting on themselves. He points out that the narcissistic person benefits from this fake identity by being able to escape the vulnerability and uncertainty that accompany feelings of personal inadequacy or desire.

#: Narcissistic Pain And Self-Delusion

A leading authority on narcissism and communication, Preston Ni teaches communication at Foothill College in Silicon Valley, California. He points out that the main causes of narcissism are two pathologies: narcissistic wound and narcissistic indulgence.

Self-centered Injury

Preston Ni shares Dr. Meyers' belief that an individual with a tendency toward narcissism becomes narcissistic when they go through "something" that makes them feel unworthy. In an attempt to heal the wound of feeling inadequate—what Professor Ni refers to as a narcissistic wound—the individual fabricates a false identity to cover up their weakness.

He points out that the majority of narcissistic wounds have their roots in difficult early experiences, whether they be social or familial. The lecturer goes on to say that narcissistic behavior arises when someone with low self-esteem faces pressure from society and familial conflict during early life.

For instance, a narcissistically inclined individual may fabricate a false identity to comfort themselves in the aftermath of a narcissistic trauma, which may cause them to feel inadequate, injured, or ashamed.

Professor Ni continues, "A narcissistically inclined person adopts compensatory schemes because of the occurrence of narcissistic wounds, which are the cause of narcissism." Rather than cultivating resilience, the individual develops grandiosity, an alter ego, a false sense of self, and other narcissistic qualities.

Narcissists have unstable personalities because, as Professor Ni and other mental health experts have pointed out, developing this alter ego is incredibly ineffective. This weakness, coupled with a persistent feeling of personal inadequacy, is what keeps narcissistic behavior going.

Self-centered Overindulgence

Professor Ni points out that narcissistic indulgence also forms in early childhood, much like narcissistic wounds. When someone close to someone with low self-esteem engages in actions that make them feel "special" or "better than," this is known as a narcissistic indulgence.

A narcissistic personality is most likely to develop, for instance, when parents and other family members overindulge a child's whims and make him or her feel "incapable of doing any wrong."

Like Professor Ni, the majority of mental health professionals concur that early childhood excesses are a major contributor to narcissistic tendencies, particularly in young adults.

That agreement makes sense since a moldable youngster may develop an inflated ego if parental, social, and cultural circumstances persuade them to believe they are better than others or should receive special treatment.

Many of these experts concur that there is nothing wrong with giving a child praise. However, they also point out that giving in to criticism and allowing a child to get away with anything is bad since it encourages entitlement, a quality that most narcissists share.

The development of indulgent, narcissistic tendencies is fostered when [any] condition makes a child feel that he or she is the exception to the rule, a unique, exceptional individual deserving of extraordinary benefits. Additionally, it makes the offending child think that there are no consequences for using and mistreating others—after all, "superior" beings can get away with doing whatever they want, don't they?

Adopting such a belief system in a youngster causes him or her to feel entitled to pampering, which breeds narcissistic, indulgent behaviors (indulgent narcissism). Youngsters like this feel that they are the center of the universe and believe that "walking on air" or "being pedestalized" is something they are entitled to.

As a result, such a child is prone to grow into a narcissistic shell, as noted by Professor Ni.

Despite its haughty exterior, this shell serves as a protective barrier for a weak self-image that cannot endure without outside approval.

Based on his research, Professor Ni thinks that the main causes of inclinations in otherwise healthy persons are narcissistic indulgences and narcissistic hurts. He points out that the main causes of the manipulation, lack of empathy, and self-absorption associated with narcissistic personality disorder are these two realities.

Section Six

Handling

Medication for narcissism should not be used unless there are other mental health conditions, such as anxiety or depression. Psychotherapy is used to treat the illness. However, if additional mental illnesses are present, it's critical to treat them with antidepressants or tranquilizers. If these additional mental health issues are not resolved, the patient cannot react well to psychotherapy techniques. The treatment's objective is to identify dysfunctional thought patterns, beliefs, and behaviors and, if necessary, minimize or completely eradicate them. Then, healthier thought patterns will progressively take their place.

Group and Family Counseling

Family and group therapy sessions may be part of this process because they serve as the cornerstone of relationships and are frequently the most conducive to recovery. After all, NPD is mostly concerned with relationship issues, right? Healthy relationship-building requires interaction with a variety of people. If children are involved, one advantage of family engagement is the potential to break the cycle and take all necessary precautions to ensure that the issue is not passed on to subsequent generations.

If successful, the process can take several years and require difficult lifestyle adjustments. One can't lead an "all about me" lifestyle forever.

In the Modern World, Narcissism

Regarding narcissism, there are a few themes and patterns that you may see. In today's world, personality disorders like this one are growing increasingly widespread. Nonetheless, it is observed that in contrast to the Eastern world, it is more prominent in the Western world.

Research that was done on both West and East Germany can support this. Participants in the controlled trial came from identical demographic backgrounds on either side. The findings indicated that whereas East Germans had better self-esteem, West Germans were more narcissistic. This demonstrates that the narcissistic epidemic is not directly affecting every region of the world. Germany's East and West are not even geographically distinct regions. They belong to a larger whole. But there's another way of thinking that impacts the narcissistic populace.

Common Modern Narcissistic Signs

The modern mind has been so ingrained with some ideas that it no longer considers them to be strange:

- Memes, song lyrics, Instagram photographs, tweets, and postings that are only about the self Books that are self-published or written by publishers with an emphasis on the self
- Lyrics to songs that celebrate the "I" and its improvement, success, and liberty

Others contend that the current state of affairs results from the widespread existence of individuals who lack self-belief. The rate of low self-esteem is rising. If you've spent the entire day admiring and enviously glancing over social media, how can you not feel like an awful person? A small part of you tells yourself that most items are only decorative. People discuss the best moments of their lives and share their best photos. When they're upset, they post about how powerful they are and how they can overcome their anger. The need to validate oneself is a healthy urge. But the constant barrage of the same ideas gradually shapes an extremely egotistical culture.

You will also need to analyze yourself when you reach the last few chapters of this book. By then, you could begin to doubt some qualities this contemporary society has bestowed upon you. Is it a good thing or a bad thing? The irony in this situation is that the society you are meant to be actively collaborating with and a part of may also be the source of the tools you need to turn self-centered and selfish. The examples you see of celebrities and other well-known individuals may be the ones who first exposed you to your narcissistic side. Why, after all, can you not emulate the affluent football players, published authors, movie stars, and skillful politicians? Aren't the things they're displaying success formulas? And you wouldn't mind having some of that?

Various Narcissist Types

The Narcissist: The Vulnerable and Invulnerable

prone to vulnerability. These narcissists are the ones who have gone through difficult situations. They are typically quiet individuals who are highly self-conscious and difficult to trust. But because of their painful history, which has led to a dread of rejection as well as an abandonment phobia, they are unable to receive love or care for others or feel the same emotions. They are emotionally guarded individuals who have created emotional barriers to protect themselves despite being sensitive and easily hurt. As a result, they present a false impression of themselves to others. The weak narcissist wants to believe this, too, to some level. They experience internalized sentiments of worthlessness, believing themselves unworthy and incapable. This translates into their extraordinary capacity for deceit, manipulation, and pulling strings. They tend to demand pity and undivided attention, guilt-trip other people, and avoid calling you out and shaming you. They are unable to recognize your worth, either.

Untouchable. These people are the well-known kind of narcissistic folks. They are cunning, arrogant, conceited, and self-assured individuals who should be avoided at all costs. They consider themselves to be a gift to humanity. They exhibit complete contempt for your feelings, emotions, and circumstances, much like weak narcissists do. They are condescending people who frequently leave us feeling so irritated that we can no longer believe someone could be so self-absorbed, egotistical, and self-centered towards us and others. Authoritative personalities with an avaricious desire to rule and control everything are known as invulnerable narcissists. They believe they have a right to be a leader because they have a superiority complex. They lack a filter and aspire to be the brightest person in the room. One aspect of having no filter is that it gives the impression that they lack empathy; they are heartless and seem to dismiss criticism as unimportant.

Narcissistic Elitist

These people are entitled and think they are superior to everyone else. The only reason these narcissists have achieved so much in life is because they have pushed you aside in order to get where they are. These are not cooperative people, whether as friends, partners, or in business. They will take great pride in everything they have accomplished. Because of the attention they have had, they believe they are unique, and they somewhat anticipate that everyone will notice their accolades, accomplishments, or other accomplishments.

Evil-minded Narcissist

This is by far the most hazardous kind of narcissist, frequently linked to drug use and sales, gang-related activities, and criminal behavior. They have no morality at all and are almost psychotic. Both good and bad things are good. Being extremely frightening and threatening, they lack the basic human emotion of kindness due to their arrogance, aggression, and lack of emotional filter for whatever they have done wrong. Where are these folks going to be? As treatment centers and prisons.

A passionate narcissist

These people are sexual narcissists. A few of us are familiar with one. They constantly boast about their sex experiences, either with each other or about themselves. They may be described as excessively sexual and perverted. Moreover, materialistic, amorous narcissists are frequently delusional about wealth—we refer to them as money-grabbers and golddiggers. Their attractiveness makes it easy for them to convince and entice you to discover what they truly have their eye on. They are the "I'll call you back" and "one-night stand" individuals. They are sensual, exhibitionist people.

Confident Narcissist

that you should just consider their opinion, which is the correct one. Although it can be annoying, this is just how they are. Whether it's someone in our family or someone at work, we all know someone who is an obnoxious narcissist. These views can cover various topics, from managing your finances to suggesting a brand of cologne or shampoo.

Shameful Narcissist

This is the type of narcissist you encounter in any setting, including offices and classrooms. They are the ones who take great satisfaction in their abilities to degrade and undermine you; they are the bullies. They act this way automatically while also making an impression on their friends—their "groupies."

Reimbursing Narcissist

These narcissists have a pessimistic view of themselves. Despite their many flaws, they purposefully use deception to hide them. They are frustrated people. What is referred to as aggressively passive.

Exuberant Narcissist

These narcissists are persons who, as the title above implies, are excessively arrogant about their accomplishments and successes. They want everyone to be aware of their amazing qualities.

Become fully radicalized, resulting in a unique point of view. Millions of individuals worldwide experience this. However, why is this disease so significant? Essentially, it has a greater impact on others than on narcissists. It's an "I'm great, but you're not so much" disease that affects both parties mentally. However, distinguishing narcissists from other people is a whole other category that we ought to investigate.

Connections. One need that people have is for connection. While a narcissist do require healthy connection and the interaction that accompanies it, the "true nature" that lurks within them makes it difficult for them to maintain genuine intimate relationships. The actual essence of a narcissist is the power to rob another person of their color. We may know that narcissistic individuals do not care about our sentiments. However, those of us who have been in relationships with narcissists have inside knowledge of the mental processes that they go through. We also experience the same suffering, hopelessness, and frequently melancholy emotions when we realize how much time we have wasted on them. They rob us of our vitality and use us.

Low self-esteem in narcissists can be easily linked to their upbringing and past experiences.

The physical and mental violence they experienced as children. They appear so self-conscious of their imperfections that they put on a "different face" every day to hide them. What, though, are they lacking? Compassion.

Section Three

Recognizing Selfish Behaviour: 14 Indicators & Symptoms

At its core, narcissism is an inordinate sense of pride and arrogance. In order to create a superiority complex and have scant regard for other people, narcissists stretch the boundaries of certainty. Living with or loving someone who demonstrates narcissistic traits is challenging. A spouse may need to wait several months before realizing that something is off due to the deceitful nature of narcissists. By then, people can have already come to terms with narcissistic abuse and be past the point of healing.

What constitutes maltreatment by narcissists?

Narcissus abuse is a specific type of maltreatment perpetrated by narcissists. Usually, it appears as though one partner is using the other for personal gain. It's a means of bonding when one manipulates and denigrates the other. The narcissist's goal is to keep their spouse dependent on admiration and consumed with their desires, whether by extreme or covert dominance. When confronted by their spouse, they deny any wrongdoing and then reverse the situation so that the victim is now held accountable for whatever appeared to be violent.

When this happens often, the victim questions their nature, intuition, and veracity. In addition to financial, scheduling, friendship, and opinion dominance, there could be domestic violence. The nonabusive partner is frequently called names, has their reasons examined, and receives guidance on responding. The abusive partner may justify their actions by citing their good intentions.

The causes for narcissism.

Research on the behaviorism of narcissism indicates that, despite the variety of behaviors exhibited by narcissists, this kind of self-importance frequently stems from a pervasive sense of guilt. Maybe a person is trying to escape a painful past that makes them feel small or weak, or they may be disguising a behavioral or physical flaw in an unhealthy way. Narcissism is frequently the result of experiences in childhood. You may have thought other people would care for you the same way because your parents either ignored you or raised you to cater to everyone's whims. There is also the hypothesis that those who were abused or denigrated as children would have carried over and accepted these behaviors into their adult relationships.

Others assert that it is simple to identify narcissism in people who possess the means and power to isolate themselves, that is, in people who have sufficient control over their environment to restrict their interactions with those who could provide them helpful feedback. However, pathological neediness or the act of feigning to be someone else's victim can also be symptoms of an overwhelming desire to control the discourse or disregard other people's feelings.

Narcissism is indeed difficult to recognize. Diagnostics used in medicine cannot find it.

Abuse of narcissistic syndrome

Syndrome of mistreatment by narcissists: They lose the ability to distinguish between their thoughts and those of the abuser. They could struggle to recognize the abuser's lies even if they have evidence of them. Victims come to blindly obey their abusive partner without challenging or considering their ideas.

It is common to feel physically, mentally, psychologically, and emotionally exhausted from a relationship with a narcissist. Some people may have physical pain from long-term stress, including severe sleeplessness, stomach problems, and anxiety-related outbursts or trigger responses.

Recovering from toxic or narcissistic relationships takes time. You feel vulnerable, uneasy, and mistrustful. If you are experiencing any or all of these signs, you are healing from a toxic relationship. With the assistance of a licensed therapist, you might gradually make progress.

Be mindful of these cautionary indicators.

Here are some specific tactics narcissists may employ to maintain control over their victims. The severity and order of these acts may vary depending on how far the abuser is willing to go in order to accomplish their objectives. Psychopaths seem to enjoy seeing other people suffer, whereas narcissists simply enjoy accomplishing their objectives. Even if they might not enjoy the situations they generate, they might not even know how awful they are. Once their main goal has been accomplished, abusive behaviors may cease, only to recur when a new problem arises.

Be mindful of these early warning signs:

1. controllingbehavior

Controlling behavior is more common in those with narcissistic personality disorder. They may initially appear to only seek control over their partner's affection and attention, but over time, they will begin to want more. They might even try to convince their partner to exclusively do activities that will benefit or delight the narcissist. They might even insist that their preferences be followed. Even though most dominating behaviors are subtle, they are all noticeable. In order to maintain control over others, narcissists frequently fabricate, mislead, or conceal information. To narcissists, authority is the same as power.

2. inward concentration

Narcissistic abusers tend to be conceited and self-centered. They deceive others into giving them intense attention through various behaviors ranging from humorous to hostile. Some violent deeds have such power that they stun others. Sometimes, they are frightening. Narcissists, in any event, don't care whom they have to place on a pedestal in order to be viewed favorably. They are also well known for exhibiting unpredictable emotions, which guarantees that their victim is well aware of the narcissist's feelings and devotes a great deal of effort to predicting their whims and desires.

3. Gaslighting

Therapists describe gaslighting as a type of deception intended to confuse. This strategy is employed to make someone else question their existence. One can cast doubt on other people's opinions and memories or act as though they have forgotten or are unaware of an incident in which they had a major part. The major goal of this approach is to continue to hold a dominant position concerning others. The narcissist's interpretation of reality will win out if they can convince others that their opinions or memories are false. Once they have control over the narrative, they believe they can use that control to affect outcomes in their favor.

4. Being cut off from society

Narcissistic abusers frequently utilize isolation attempts as a lead-up to more serious forms of abuse. The narcissist destroys the victim's supporting relationships, including those with friends, family, and social media, since they believe they are the primary source of love, praise, and encouragement. Keeping a victim hidden from the eyes of people closest to them, who know them best, may also allow an abuser more time to gain control over the victim.

When the victim's family or friends show worry for their narcissistic spouse or ask how much the victim has changed while living with them, the narcissist will try to keep the victim from seeing them. The narcissist may also deceive their spouse or speak poorly about their partner's relatives to stop them from forming or maintaining plans with other people. They might even invent disputes or emergencies.

Victims report feeling confused about social norms after being cut off for an extended period. A victim who has become accustomed to controlling methods may be unaware of how to behave "correctly" with other people. This could show the narcissist avoiding persons they think could be hazardous or acting aloof in social circumstances. Since they have no other supportive relationships outside of those with the abuser, the victim experiences social isolation.

5. making people who are not in the connection unreliable

Being by oneself inevitably breeds suspicion of other people. Narcissists frequently invent facts or take advantage of delicate situations to position themselves as their victim's most reliable source of information. As a result, victims frequently turn to their abusers to confirm the "reality of the situation" or to ascertain whether the surroundings are "secure." Narcissists may also actively sow doubt in the victim's mind about previously reliable family members, law enforcement officials, and professionals whose viewpoints differ from their own.

6. Invasion of privacy on the internet

Countless victims also mention technical obstacles like tracking devices, internet restrictions, or password theft. Sometimes, physical isolation is required, like when someone leaves their home nation or state.

These invasions of privacy on the internet could be just as disturbing and damaging as physical isolation. Abusers may even go so far as to create a false online persona and communicate with their victims in order to confirm their loyalty. They might even threaten to publish sensitive content online, including images or intimate photos. Invasion of the victim's online privacy is just one of several coercive tactics employed to ensure total dependence and collaboration.

7. abusive language

Narcissists use derogatory language and putdowns to make sure their victims never trust their judgments. *Abuse* is defined as any behavior that is meant to degrade or humiliate another person, even if it is occasionally subtle. It's possible to make unpleasant comments about someone's appearance or decisions in a lighthearted way or while pretending to be supportive. The most horrific kind of emotional assault results from verbal sniping. Slandering, berating, and criticizing others can be replaced with threats, yelling, and mental agony. Furthermore, verbally abusive situations have the potential to be violent, even in the absence of physical contact. Narcissists frequently grow entitled to their suffering, which gives them an excuse to torture and mistreat others.

8. employing physical force as a warning

Even though the main aim of narcissistic abuse is frequently emotional control, these abusers can also damage property, hurt other people— or attempt to hurt others—or harm themselves as a kind of punishment or to make a partner fearful. Remember, narcissists are attention-seekers. They may become more aggressive and forceful when you can no longer persuade them. Their pride and exaggerated sense of self-worth coexist, and their inability to regulate their emotions can lead to frightening events, blackmail, and violent outbursts.

9. Vacuuming

A form of emotional manipulation known as "hoovering," narcissistic abusers frequently use it. This strategy was called after the vacuum cleaner industry and pulled the victim back into a vicious cycle of abuse. When abusers believe they are losing control, they may go into a cycle of making things better. This could show up as a complete acknowledgment of the victim's feelings or as a lifting of previous restrictions on social interactions and routines. Nonetheless, this refractory stage is typically brief. The abuser gains the victim's trust, and soon, the episode of social exclusion and power resumes.

Breaking Free: Taking Back Your Identity

Could you answer this question, "Who are you really?" with assurance and hesitancy if I asked you right now? Do you know who you are at your heart, below all the masks you wear, your roles, and the labels others have given you? One of the strongest foundations we may have is our identity. Without it, we open ourselves up to other people's influence, especially narcissists and other people who use manipulative techniques.

And why is our fight against narcissism so dependent on identity? Since the narcissist seeks to infiltrate and seize control at this center, this epicenter of "self," You are shielded from these attempts at dominance and control by a strong identity. Do you recognize this? Should you have perused Chapter 4, you will fully understand my meaning.

Several of the most accomplished intellectuals of our day have studied the complexities of identification. In "Identity" (2004), Zigmund Bauman states that "the search for personal identity is, in reality, the search for freedom." This is a sentence that, after some thought, has a very deep resonance for anyone who has felt the oppressive pressure of a narcissistic relationship.

Consider it. How many times have you felt that you were sacrificing who you were to win someone over or blend in? How often have you given up on your goals, aspirations, and morals to maintain harmony or win someone else's approval? You're in the correct spot if any of these terms ring a bell.

Now, allow me to pose a quick question to you before I go any further: Have you ever taken a moment to consider a caterpillar going through a transformation? It defends itself within its cocoon, disintegrates entirely, and reemergesas a new creature with wings and freedom from that seeming chaos. What if I told you that you, too, can break free from the bonds that have held you back and, like that caterpillar, evolve into the person you truly are?

Identity is elusive even if it is vital. It alters, adapts, and evolves continuously as we mature and go through life. Therefore, don't panic if you've lost your sense of self. It's entirely typical. Furthermore, it is reversible. You may rediscover who you are and reestablish a connection with your essence if you have the correct resources and information.

So, how can we set out on this path of self-discovery and identity reclamation? A map is necessary for this trip, just like for any other. I will provide you with that map in this chapter.

We will begin by figuring out and dispelling the myths and limiting beliefs you have created for yourself or that other people have ingrained in you. Recall that in Chapter 2, we discussed

NLP's hidden role. We shall revisit it, as it will prove to be an invaluable instrument at this stage of your expedition. Next, we will discuss strategies for fortifying and safeguarding your identity, ensuring that the actions of a narcissist can never again rock your foundation.

Additionally, never forget that you are not alone during this journey if you ever feel lost or overwhelmed. I'm here to help, and together, we will regain your identity—something that is naturally yours—step by step.

It is important to understand that outside factors frequently distort our sense of who we are as we go closer to rediscovering who we are. Just for a moment, picture a mirror. A mirror that is used to reflect your image but has accumulated dust and fingerprints over time. Until you take the time to clean it, you can't see properly, right? Likewise, the alterations forced upon us by others may conceal our true selves.

In her seminal work "You Can Heal Your Life" (1984), Louise Hay emphasized the significance of loving ourselves and releasing ourselves from the unfavorable thoughts we have been taught. According to Hay's theory, early experiences and other people's remarks can permanently influence our self-perception. The brilliant thing about his strategy is that he also acknowledges our ability to alter those beliefs and swap them out for more positive and accurate ones.

We have already studied Neuro-Linguistic Programming (NLP) in earlier chapters, and it provides effective methods for doing this. Finding and replacing the "negative affirmations" we have internalized is one of the most powerful tactics. These self-affirmations are essentially the narratives we tell ourselves about our identities, worth, and potential.

Together, let's engage in a little exercise. Please consider a self-defeating belief you may have. It could be something you've been told repeatedly by a narcissist in your life, or it could be something you believe based on events from the past. Have you got it? Now think about how you feel about that belief: Dense? Restricted? Captured?

I want you to then rewrite that notion in a way that gives you more authority. The importance of an environment that fosters growth and self-discovery was emphasized by Carl Rogers, one of the most well-known psychologists of the 20th century and the author of "The Process of Becoming a Person" (1961). For instance, if the belief is "I'm not good enough," you can replace it with "I have inherent value and am capable of achieving whatever I set my mind to." He claimed that people can better identify and behave by their genuine selves when they feel understood and appreciated.

The problem now is that you have most likely not been in that setting if a narcissist has influenced you. The good news is that it's something you can make yourself. You will also see that you can always determine who you are, independent of other people's beliefs or influences, as you start to see clearly through the distortions.

However, bravery is needed for this process. It calls on you to confront the dark, to silence the voices of the past, and to gradually reconstruct a strong and true self-image. It is a trip with ups and downs, like any other journey. But I can assure you that the benefits of emotional freedom and sincerity will outweigh every step along the way.

If you can, picture a grand old building. It was once the envy of many, but with time, it has become abandoned, and its walls display indications of deterioration. But you choose to repair it rather than demolish it. You gradually remove the layers of aging paint, strengthen the structure's foundation, and ensure that each brick is properly placed. What was once a forgotten building is restored to its former splendor with time and effort.

Regaining your identity is a similar therapeutic process. It entails removing the layers of harmful influence and starting again with a strong, sincere base. It's also one of the most satisfying tasks you can do, while not easy.